Greetings
from
ALABAMA

Greetings from
ALABAMA

Greetings
from
ALABAMA

Greetings from
ALABAMA

Greetings
from
ALABAMA

Greetings from
ALABAMA

Greetings from
ALABAMA

Greetings from
ALABAMA

Greetings from
ALABAMA

Greetings from
ALABAMA

Greetings from
ALABAMA

Greetings from
ALABAMA

Greetings from
ALABAMA

Greetings from
ALABAMA

Greetings
from
ALABAMA

Greetings from
ALABAMA

Greetings from
ALABAMA

Greetings
from
ALABAMA

Greetings from
ALABAMA

Greetings
from
ALABAMA

Greetings
from
ALABAMA

Greetings from
ALABAMA

Greetings from
ALABAMA

Greetings from
ALABAMA

Greetings from
ALABAMA

Greetings from
ALABAMA

Greetings from
ALABAMA

Greetings from
ALABAMA

Greetings from
ALABAMA

Greetings from
ALABAMA

Greetings
from
ALABAMA

Greetings from
ALABAMA

Greetings from
ALABAMA

Greetings from
ALABAMA

Greetings from
ALABAMA

Greetings from
ALABAMA

Greetings
from
ALABAMA

Greetings from
ALABAMA

Greetings from
ALABAMA

Greetings from
ALABAMA

Greetings from
ALABAMA

Greetings from
ALABAMA

Greetings from
ALABAMA

Greetings from
ALABAMA

Greetings
from
ALABAMA

Greetings from
ALABAMA

Greetings from
ALABAMA

Greetings from
ALABAMA

Greetings from
ALABAMA

Greetings
from
ALABAMA

Greetings from
ALABAMA

Greetings from
ALABAMA

Greetings
from
ALABAMA

Greetings
from
ALABAMA

Greetings
from
ALABAMA

Greetings from
ALABAMA

Greetings from
ALABAMA

Greetings
from
ALABAMA

Greetings from
ALABAMA

Greetings from
ALABAMA

Greetings from
ALABAMA

Greetings from
ALABAMA

Greetings from
ALABAMA

Greetings from
ALABAMA

Greetings from
ALABAMA

Greetings from
ALABAMA

Greetings
from
ALABAMA

Greetings from
ALABAMA

Greetings from
ALABAMA

Greetings from
ALABAMA

Greetings
from
ALABAMA

Greetings from
ALABAMA

Greetings from
ALABAMA

Greetings from
ALABAMA

Greetings from
ALABAMA

Printed in the USA
CPSIA information can be obtained
at www.ICGtesting.com
CBHW031314160724
11668CB00009B/350

9 798385 400379